In this mini-b
experience int
from. Writing \
comfort, she offers a practical framework for engaging traumatized people wisely and well. If you care for someone whose life has been disrupted by the impact of trauma, you'll benefit greatly from reading this resource.

—**Christine Chappell**, Author, *Midnight Mercies*;
    Host, *Hope + Help Podcast*, Institute for Biblical
    Counseling & Discipleship

So many Christians who have undergone traumatic suffering want to experience church as a place of help and healing. But in order for that to happen, church leaders and friends need wisdom and training. Darby has served us well toward this goal with her excellent and efficient overview of Christian trauma care.

—**Michael Gembola**, Executive Director, Blue Ridge
    Christian Counseling

This book tackles the vital, yet controversial issue of trauma: how do you help people whose souls have been put out of joint by suffering terrible evils? Biblically thoughtful, attuned to the healing role the church can play, and highly practical (including an individualizable "Finding Refuge" plan), this is an excellent companion for those ministering to souls who feel shattered.

—**Alasdair Groves**, Executive Director, Christian
    Counseling and Educational Foundation (CCEF)

Do you want to be a good friend to someone who's been through a profoundly difficult experience? In this mini-book, Darby takes you by the hand as you come alongside your friend. Darby orients you to the experience of trauma and helps you to avoid common, well-intentioned mistakes. Take the time to read this book. Your friend will thank you. You will be a better ambassador of God's comfort because you did.
—**Brad Hambrick**, Pastor of Counseling, The
    Summit Church; Author, *Angry with God*

When I face complex situations, I need the counsel of faithful friends who have traveled treacherous paths. Darby does exactly that, guiding the helper to care for those who have experienced the horror of trauma. Read and listen to the years of wisdom curated here, and then take heart in our Savior who promises his presence in the darkest of hours.
—**Jonathan D. Holmes**, Executive Director,
    Fieldstone Counseling

This helpful booklet addresses the complicated and important topic of trauma with precision, biblical truth, and wisdom. Once again, Darby Strickland helps us to apply grace and truth as we care for hurting people. I'm so thankful for this useful and needed guide for applying the Scriptures to the real world.
—**Mark Vroegop**, Lead Pastor, College Park Church,
    Indianapolis; Author, *Dark Clouds, Deep Mercy*

Trauma

Caring for Survivors

Resources for Changing Lives

A Ministry of
THE CHRISTIAN COUNSELING AND
EDUCATIONAL FOUNDATION
Glenside, Pennsylvania

RCL Ministry Booklets

Trauma

Caring for Survivors

Darby A. Strickland

P&R
PUBLISHING
P.O. BOX 817 • PHILLIPSBURG • NEW JERSEY 08865-0817

© 2023 by Darby A. Strickland

All rights reserved. No part of this book may be reproduced, stored in a retrieval system, or transmitted in any form or by any means—electronic, mechanical, photocopy, recording, or otherwise—except for brief quotations for the purpose of review or comment, without the prior permission of the publisher, P&R Publishing Company, P.O. Box 817, Phillipsburg, New Jersey 08865-0817.

Unless otherwise indicated, Scripture quotations are from the ESV® Bible (The Holy Bible, English Standard Version®), copyright © 2001 by Crossway, a publishing ministry of Good News Publishers. Used by permission. All rights reserved.

The Scripture quotation marked (CSB) has been taken from the Christian Standard Bible®, Copyright © 2017 by Holman Bible Publishers. Used by permission. Christian Standard Bible®, and CSB® are federally registered trademarks of Holman Bible Publishers.

The Scripture quotation marked (NIV) is taken from the Holy Bible, New International Version®, NIV®. Copyright © 1973, 1978, 1984, 2011 by Biblica, Inc.™ Used by permission of Zondervan. All rights reserved worldwide. www.zondervan.com. The "NIV" and "New International Version" are trademarks registered in the United States Patent and Trademark Office by Biblica, Inc.™

This booklet is adapted from Darby Strickland, "Foundations of Trauma Care for Biblical Counselors," *Journal of Biblical Counseling* 36, no. 2 (2022): 25–56. Used with permission.

Printed in the United States of America

Library of Congress Cataloging-in-Publication Data

Names: Strickland, Darby A., author.
Title: Trauma : caring for survivors / Darby Strickland.
Description: Phillipsburg, New Jersey : P&R Publishing Company, [2023] |
    Series: Resources for changing lives | Includes bibliographical
    references. | Summary: "Darby Strickland helps us to understand trauma
    and its effects-and, drawing from Psalm 121, to become trustworthy
    guides who restore sufferers to a flourishing love for God and others"–
    Provided by publisher.
Identifiers: LCCN 2023016477 | ISBN 9781629959863 (paperback) | ISBN
    9781629959870 (epub)
Subjects: LCSH: Psychic trauma–Religious aspects–Christianity. | Psychic
    trauma–Biblical teaching. | Psychic trauma–Patients–Pastoral
    counseling of. | Church work. | Bible. Psalms.
Classification: LCC BV4461 .S77 2023 | DDC 259/.42–dc23/eng/20230525
LC record available at https://lccn.loc.gov/2023016477

After Bible study, a group of young women approached me. They were deeply shaken. Their dear friend Emily[1] had been sexually assaulted by her boyfriend in a brutal attack, and when her friends had seen her afterward, she had still been bruised and in shock. Understanding the gravity of what had happened, Emily's friends wanted to help her to get counseling. They knew she would need support.

In addition to giving them some potential counselors' names, I asked the young women how they thought Emily was doing. They told me that she was not sleeping and had not seemed coherent when she told them what had happened. One friend pointed out that her face had not changed expression as she spoke about her visit to the police station: "It was like she was detached from the horror."

I wanted Emily's friends to know that her most urgent need was to be oriented to her experience—to know what to expect. It is normal for the first few days and weeks after an assault to be challenging. I explained that it might be hard for Emily to sleep and concentrate and that she might experience additional, more pronounced physical symptoms of anxiety.

I explained that this was the time for her friends to grieve with her, not to ask Emily questions or to press her to reveal more than she was comfortable with sharing. She probably wouldn't be able to focus on what they were saying anyway. Instead, it would be healing for Emily if they wept and lamented with her. Their presence would be more important for her than any words.

And I explained that Emily also needed to know one simple truth: the attack was not her fault.

Carefully planning for and addressing the impacts of trauma requires a wealth of wisdom. The suffering of traumatized people like Emily is significant, and they are easy to wound further if we do not engage with them thoughtfully and intentionally. As we will see, caring for people who have been traumatized is complex. After a brief overview of trauma and its symptoms and challenges, this booklet will focus on the *foundations* of trauma care: (1) addressing the overwhelming impacts of a survivor's trauma, (2) stabilizing the survivor, and (3) helping the survivor to build trust with you before you delve into the intimate details of their story and struggle. Whether you are a professional counselor, someone in church ministry, or a concerned friend, there are ways you can help.

What Is Trauma?

The word *trauma* refers to the emotional, spiritual, and physical disruptions that occur when a person is overwhelmed by extreme suffering. People use the word *traumatized* to describe a person who has been severely impacted by a terrible event—such as rape, a natural disaster, or a car accident. An event may rise to the level of a traumatic experience when it is sudden and unpredictable, involves a threat to life, or is a profound violation of trust. The word *traumatized* also describes a person who is overwhelmed after a series of adverse experiences—such as occurs in childhood abuse, war, or domestic violence. Traumatized people often experience a severe disruption in their relationships with God and others because of what has happened.

With that description of trauma in mind, let me make a few clarifications. Not everyone who experiences a horrible event will be traumatized by it. And for those who are, some will have symptoms that resolve after a few weeks, while others will wrestle with long-term effects. Although symptoms of trauma often share similarities, individual responses to events can vary widely.

Trauma care is therefore challenging because it requires us to attune ourselves to the specific needs of an individual and to discover how *they themselves* have responded to and processed their experiences. As we encounter individuals who

3

have been traumatized, we must ask, "What do I need to learn, understand, and know about the experience of trauma before I care for this tender soul? How has the person in front of me been affected by trauma? And how does Scripture speak to their heart and situation?" To do so is to be both trauma informed and biblical.

Trauma Informed and Scripture Informed

At its core, to be *trauma informed* means to be familiar with the signs and symptoms of trauma and to understand its vast impact on a person. The information on trauma that helps us to do this comes out of the important observations many professionals (such as police officers, teachers, social workers, counselors, and doctors) have made about its effect on the people they serve.

When I first heard the term *trauma informed*, I thought, "Why would I want *trauma* to inform my care? I want the Bible to inform my care!" And rightly so. We need to be on guard against taking on a worldview that is centered around trauma. Although secular therapists and other professionals are correctly concerned about people's suffering, they do not view people as image bearers who live, body and soul, before the living God. Because their anthropology is inaccurate, their understanding of the problem—and its solution—will not point others toward true hope: the gospel. And though trauma is important to understand, it cannot be the sole or principal lens by which we understand suffering people. Rather, Scripture's perspectives on human suffering, sin, and redemption should control how we understand traumatic experiences and approach survivors.

At the same time, there is tremendous value in being trauma informed—in reading widely to understand the impacts and effects of trauma on a person. Literature on trauma encapsulates key research and a wealth of case studies that help us to see impacts of trauma that are not immediately apparent. When I consulted secular research on trauma, it confirmed the very things I was noticing as I worked with survivors and provided keen observations and descriptions that helped me when I encountered challenging counseling cases.

The more I learned from studying traumatized people and trauma literature, the more I had to wrestle with the complexity of body-soul suffering. This pushed me back into Scripture, and I probed God's Word more deeply to find robust and biblical conceptualizations that would give me hopeful ways to minister to sufferers.

The goal of our study—of Scripture and of other literature—is to be able to make case-specific, biblical applications for traumatized individuals and to bring God's words of comfort to refresh weary, troubled souls. Thus, to be trauma informed does not mean we need to understand or agree with everything that has been written about trauma in secular literature. But the information on trauma that we gather helps us to be better stewards of the people God has placed in our care (1 Peter 4:10) as we reinterpret it through a biblical lens.

Ultimately, the goals of biblical counseling should compel us to learn more about trauma and how it has impacted the people we are working with. Good biblical counseling involves carefully mining the Scriptures so that we can speak to a person's situation and condition, acknowledging that we are embodied souls whose bodies may need just as much support as our souls do, understanding that community plays a vital role in healing, recognizing that the human heart actively interprets the world and its experiences and needs to be guided to interpret it well, knowing that God's pursuit of each person is highly personal and so our care must be as well, and addressing faith questions that arise in a season of suffering. Now, that is a long list! But this is how we are called to love people under our care, and stewarding what we learn about trauma through a biblical lens can help us to fulfill this calling.

Trauma in Scripture

Helpers are most helpful when they have a basic knowledge of trauma and the many ways it impacts a person.[2] As we consider how Scripture can inform our care, we'll turn to the book of Job for a useful overview of symptoms that commonly result from extreme suffering. Job's reaction to losing his family, possessions, and health serves as a guide for understanding what survivors of trauma experience.

Physical Anguish

Job's suffering is visceral. He has trouble eating. "I refuse to touch it; such food makes me ill" (Job 6:7 NIV). And he has trouble sleeping. "When I lie down I say, 'When shall I arise?' But the night is long, and I am full of tossing till the dawn" (7:4).

Shame

Job's friends label him an ungodly hypocrite, leaving him full of shame and confusion as he faces their reproach and rejection. "If I am guilty, woe to me! If I am in the right, I cannot lift up my head, for I am filled with disgrace and look on my affliction" (Job 10:15). Job's experience illustrates one form of shame, but shame can also come from people's thoughts about themselves. Trauma often leaves people feeling unworthy and unlovable, believing the traumatic event was their fault or feeling ashamed that they are still struggling to heal.

Faith Questions

Job's suffering leads him to believe that God is hostile toward him. "How long will you not look away from me, nor leave me alone till I swallow my spit?" (Job 7:19). He cannot fathom how God's justice squares with his circumstances. He does not know how to make things right with God. "If I sin, what do I do to you, you watcher of mankind? Why have you made me your mark? Why have I become a burden to you? Why do you not pardon my transgression and take away my iniquity?" (7:20–21).

Hypervigilance

After losing so much, Job fears what tragedy might come next.

> For the thing that I fear comes upon me,
>   and what I dread befalls me.
> I am not at ease, nor am I quiet;
>   I have no rest, but trouble comes. (Job
>   3:25–26)

Intrusive Thoughts and Emotions

Even when Job seeks rest, his mind fills with frightful thoughts and terrifying flashbacks.

> For the arrows of the Almighty are in me;
>   my spirit drinks their poison;
>   the terrors of God are arrayed against
>   me. (Job 6:4)

> When I say, "My bed will comfort me,
>   my couch will ease my complaint,"
> then you scare me with dreams

and terrify me with visions,
 so that I would choose strangling
    and death rather than my bones. (7:13–
        15)

Avoidance

Although Job never refuses to talk about his pain, we do see his desire to die and escape life. This is the ultimate form of avoidance.

Oh that I might have my request,
    and that God would fulfill my hope,
that it would please God to crush me,
    that he would let loose his hand and
        cut me off! (Job 6:8–9)

For now I shall lie in the earth;
    you will seek me, but I shall not be.
        (7:21)

Overwhelming Emotions

Job's tears are constant. "My face is red with weeping, and on my eyelids is deep darkness" (Job 16:16). Deep lament streams uncontrollably from him: "My sighing comes instead of my bread, and my groanings are poured out like water" (3:24). His agony is loud, deep, and abundant.

This small collection of verses from the book of Job paints a vivid picture of the impacts of deep suffering. We see from them that the effects of trauma are significant. We also see that they are not signs of unbelief but rather that they reveal what an overwhelmed body and soul sound like.

Unique Challenges in Trauma Care

As we begin to engage with a person who has endured trauma, we must be mindful of four major challenges.

Challenges for the Victim

Victims of trauma often struggle to remain in the present moment. The impacts of trauma are so great that they often cause involuntary disruption in memory, emotions, conscious awareness, perception, attention, and motor control. Because the emotions and memories of a traumatic event can be so distressing, survivors may "disconnect" as a way of distancing themselves from them. As a result, a sufferer may be physically present but not engaged in the present moment. In the trauma literature, this is described as *dissociation*.

For example, a counselee of mine who was involved in a horrific machine accident seemed able to follow the conversation we were having, but he was thinking about something entirely different. He was not even aware that he had stopped listening, and it was not easy for me to pick up on his lack of attention.

When you are speaking with a victim, check in on them to see if they are actually engaging with you. Are their eyes tracking with you? Are they truly present in the conversation?

Remembering and speaking about trauma causes distress. Speaking with a sufferer about the traumatic event might seem like an obvious place to start. But if we ask someone to talk in detail about their trauma too early, it may unsettle them, and they may respond in unhelpful, harmful, or even sinful ways.

For example, when Sam began talking about the specifics of his sexual abuse, his panic attacks became more frequent. He started having night terrors and began to misuse his prescription sleep medication as a way to sleep soundly. Bob, who had worked to avoid his memories, began to drink heavily in an attempt to drown out the memories his counselor asked him to describe. While talking with her pastor, Susan realized that her parents had known about her childhood sexual abuse but deliberately chosen *not* to protect her rather than shame her abusive uncle and make the family look bad. This dissolved her trust in her support system, and she fled her family before new supports were in place, leaving her vulnerable to homelessness and poverty.

The distress caused by engaging with trauma is a significant challenge. Later on in this booklet, we'll learn how to safeguard a sufferer's response to the stress of processing trauma before we go deeper with them.

Challenges for the Helper

Rushed attempts to instill hope often add pain instead of lifting it. When we see great suffering, we want to provide hope and make the pain go away. These are good impulses (Gal. 6:2). Scripture does call us to tend to the needy, vulnerable, and weak (Matt. 25:35-40), but our desire to help sometimes propels us toward people in a way that fails to demonstrate what wounded hearts need first and foremost: *compassion and understanding.* Too often we speak truths that people are not ready to hear.

Jennifer's heart was crushed after she lost two children in a car accident. A few short weeks after the loss, members of her small group from church sent her "notes of encouragement" that were filled with Bible verses about how her suffering would be redeemed. It was not as if those verses were untrue or inapplicable. But they were poorly timed. Jennifer needed to hear words of compassion and comfort, not words that sought to correct her grief or instruct her on what she must believe about the tragedy.

We must be careful that our words speak the right truths in the right season (Prov. 15:23). We must persist with people in their seasons of darkness and lament *before* we seek to shape their responses to suffering.

Compassionate trauma care is excruciatingly slow. When you work with a trauma victim, everything feels urgent. So many of their needs feel like they should be addressed immediately, but there are usually no shortcuts, quick truths, or miracle prayers. Helping a traumatized person looks more like helping someone climb out of a valley one tiny step at a time. This is why it's helpful to think of trauma care as prepping for and being a guide on a long, challenging journey.

With this in mind, we'll turn to Psalm 121.

Up from the Valley

God draws his people up mountains to worship. He took Moses up Mount Sinai more than once. And on the same mountain where he asked Abraham to sacrifice Isaac, he built Jerusalem as his dwelling place. No matter what direction his people came from, they had to "go up" to worship at his temple. Walking through the twists and turns of the dry, rocky terrain of the Jordan Valley toward Jerusalem, the pilgrims might encounter bandits or wild animals. It was a hazard-filled and unpredictable journey.

As the Israelites traveled, they probably wondered how they would make it through each uncertain and fear-filled day. To reassure themselves of the Lord's protection, guidance, and blessing, they rehearsed words of faith along their journey. These are known as the *psalms of ascent* (Pss. 120–34).

Take the opening verses of Psalm 121.

I lift my eyes toward the mountains.
Where will my help come from?
My help comes from the LORD,
the Maker of heaven and earth.

He will not allow your foot to slip;
your Protector will not slumber. (vv. 1–3
      CSB)

In these verses, the psalmist-sojourner sees the mountains ahead and immediately realizes he needs help. He faces a long uphill journey over rough terrain. He wonders, "Who can help me?" and then quickly asserts, "I know—the Lord is my helper."

This movement out of dangerous valleys toward the temple celebration is a helpful metaphor for thinking about how the Lord cares for people who suffer—and how we can provide care for them. Psalm 121 gives both the sufferer and the helper the freedom to ask the Lord for help and to confess feeling overwhelmed and doubtful about the path ahead. Thankfully, God will help both the afflicted *and* the guide. *He* is the one who will guide the sufferer to the temple mount, where their worship of him will be restored.

These are glorious truths that we can count on as we walk with trauma survivors up and out of the valley. Hold tight to these ascent psalms. We will need to continually find strength, steadiness, and confidence from the Maker of heaven and earth. We can be confident that God will not let our feet slip (Ps. 121:3). I am thankful that he is our good, trustworthy, and ultimate Guide.

The Three Foundations of Trauma Care

What makes for a trustworthy guide on a perilous journey? Let me start with a personal story. Our family once went on an afternoon walk to climb a waterfall. My children scurried right up. But I was terrified. All I could do was think about what would happen if I slipped and fell back onto the rocks below.

A good friend was with me who knew both me and the waterfall. She knew that my knees had issues and that my left side was weaker than my right because of a car accident. She also knew the waterfall because she had climbed it dozens of times. Seeing me tremble and hearing my protests as I started, my friend began to give clear directions: "Darby, you are going to put your right hand on that hold and bring up your left knee to that wider shelf."

My friend was meticulously kind in her directions. She factored in my weaknesses as she determined and detailed the safest route. Trusting her care of me, I focused on each next step and made it to the top. I was willing to take risks climbing the waterfall because I trusted her ability to keep me safe, even when I felt vulnerable.

Successful wilderness guides carefully prepare before they take even one step onto the trail. They are familiar with the path they are traveling and the people they are guiding. They know the potential dangers, the places to find provisions and to rest, and the strengths and weaknesses of those who depend upon them.

Our initial work with trauma survivors should be similar. We need to determine what challenges lie ahead and prepare each survivor to face them well. We do this by (1) discovering the scope of a victim's trauma and its impacts, (2) assessing their safety and stability and working to improve it, and (3) building trust as their guide. These are not steps per se. They are foundational ground to cover *before* you delve into deeper issues.

It may take weeks or months for a counselor to address these three areas well. If you serve as a support person, your role in a victim's healing journey may not be as direct as a counselor's. Either way, being aware of these foundational areas will assist you as you seek to provide appropriate help.

1. Discover the Scope of the Trauma and Its Impacts

When you are providing care for a traumatized person, it is crucial that you understand the basics of their experience: what happened and how it has affected them. Like Job, many survivors of trauma are plagued with symptoms of their suffering. Panic attacks, flashbacks, overwhelming fear, or an inability to concentrate are common. In the beginning, ask enough questions to understand the broad strokes of their trauma, but keep your focus on how they are currently doing, not on all the details of their traumatic experience.

Luke came for counseling as a victim of an armed robbery at the business he owned. He was shot during the holdup, but he needed to return to work to maintain his livelihood. He felt helpless, stuck, and vulnerable. Unfortunately, I was caught off guard and unprepared for what I was hearing. I was more interested in understanding what had happened than in identifying his needs, and my questions reflected that. Thankfully, Luke was gracious enough to hang in there with my counseling, and I eventually got to what he needed because he led me there. He needed me to understand *the impact* the event had on him emotionally, spiritually, and physically.

Get a "CliffsNotes" version of the sufferer's story. Seek to gain a basic overview of the type of trauma a person endured (for example, a violent crime, childhood trauma or sexual abuse, the deaths of family members or friends, severe illness or injury, a natural disaster, or a combination of many factors, which is called *complex trauma*).[3] Reassure them that they need to share only what they are comfortable with at this point. Details of their suffering may come later, but don't press for them.

Focus on the concerns of the sufferer. Many people do not directly report the symptoms they are experiencing. This can be due to shame, lack of trust, or their own inability to grasp how deeply they have been harmed. To care well for survivors, we must be alert to the full scope of their suffering. Once we have a general sense of what they have experienced, we can ask broad questions, such as the following, to check on their current well-being:

- How has this event impacted your daily functioning? Your sleep?
- What do you sense its effect has been on you?
- What symptoms do you find intolerable to live with?
- Do you want to tell me more about what happened?
- Where would you like to start?
- Can you tell me what you fear as you think about returning to your previous routine?
- Do you have someone who is supporting you well?
- If so, what has been helpful? If not, what has been hard about how others are caring for you?

- How has your body responded to this trauma?
- How has this event affected your faith?

These questions are a gentle way to start learning more about a victim.

Although you will often need to ask such questions, sometimes a person's level of distress propels them to reveal how deeply they are being affected, even at an early stage. For example, after being assaulted by her boyfriend, Emily struggled to sleep and eat, feared she would self-harm, and avoided people. Thankfully, whenever she feared she would begin cutting, she was quick to tell her friends about it.

Respond carefully to what you hear. In the initial stage of care, a common mistake helpers make is to reduce a survivor's heart responses to the categories we are most familiar with. For instance, we may decide a fearful person is sinning by failing to trust God. Or we may observe someone who is overcome with grief and conclude that they have withdrawn from life out of laziness. Or we may wrongly assume that a sexual assault victim is wrestling with shame, because so many do, and miss that they are in denial of the event's impact. We must embrace the complexity of each person's suffering.

Recall that Job faithfully expressed his anguish, but his friends harshly—and wrongfully

(Job 42:7-8)—judged his responses to extreme suffering. We do not want to be like them and question a sufferer's faith. Instead, we must recognize it is not a sin to be in agony—it is a normal response to tragedy. Rather than over-spiritualizing expressions of anguish, we should be willing to enter into these hard places with tenderness.

We must also embrace the time it takes for a survivor to work through what they have experienced. We understandably want to offer hope and help no matter our role. But we must remember there is no quick fix for trauma. No simple truths can make everything instantly better. If we fail to take this into account, we will re-wound people who are already suffering. For instance, Luke's church elder told him if he wanted to restore inner peace, he needed to trust God more and forgive the man who had shot him. Those were not the two truths he needed to hear at the start of his journey. At that moment, the advice felt condemning and impossible to follow.

In sum, pursue two goals at the outset of your care: understanding (1) the basic contours of the trauma and (2) its impacts on the person's body, emotions, relationships with others, and spiritual health. Rather than being driven by curiosity about a traumatic event, be driven by genuine care for the sufferer. As you speak with the person, respond carefully to what they have to say.

Ultimately, you may realize that you do not possess the skills and experience that you need to fully assess a person's trauma or help them to work through it. Even so, you can still be a great comfort to them and provide initial steps of care. If you are not a trained counselor, for example, you can help to connect the sufferer to someone who can formally assess how the person is responding to the trauma. If you discover the person is currently in danger, you may be able to play a role in getting them to safety. You can also validate the severity of their suffering by affirming the impact of what happened and pointing out their need for wise, prolonged care and counsel.

2. Assess and Establish Safety and Stability

As we discover the scope of a trauma and its impacts on a victim, we must also ask questions to assess their safety and stability. This is the second crucial foundation of trauma-informed care. Sharing about intense suffering, thus bringing evil into the light (Eph. 5:11), takes tremendous courage. The more aware you are of a victim's current situation and how they respond to distress, the better you will be able to prepare them for the hard work ahead. You do not want to start someone on a hazardous journey they are unprepared or ill-positioned to handle.

Tend to the person's injuries. If you are among the first helpers to come to a victim's assistance, do not assume their physical injuries have been addressed, especially if they have been sexually assaulted. Be sure to ask if they need medical attention or your support in pursuing medical care. Brainstorm who might accompany them to a doctor or help them to set up an appointment. You may also help them to draft a brief statement that they can share with their doctor so they do not have to tell the whole story of what happened or what needs attention.

Assess whether their environment is safe. Is the person you are helping removed from the harmful situation that traumatized them? For instance, many victims of domestic abuse still share a bed with the person who is violating them. Those who remain in dangerous situations while addressing their trauma find it nearly impossible to heal because they are simultaneously being subjected to ongoing abuse. In addition, complications increase when a victim is seeking to address domestic violence that they are experiencing while children are in the home. Take great care to help them to think through their own safety as well as that of their children.[4] Keep in mind too that if child abuse is occurring, a report needs to be made.

Sometimes the best thing you can do for the victim is to help them to secure a safe place to live, as they may encounter barriers they do not know how to overcome (money, moving, hard conversations). Look for ways to help them to problem solve, and offer practical help. This is a tangible way to bless them in a season when they are overwhelmed. If a trauma victim lives in an unsafe environment and (assuming they are an adult) they choose to remain, think carefully about how to address their trauma. Victims of ongoing trauma or abuse often have not fully grasped the extent to which they are being sinned against. The more they come to understand that they are being mistreated and harmed, the more their level of distress tends to rise. Sometimes their reactions are not carefully thought out and become problematic.

Katie was thirty-three and still living with her parents. They were spiritually abusive, and she was just coming to terms with how cruel and controlling they had been. As she became aware of their manipulations, she wanted to engage them by explaining that they were more domineering than loving. This came from a place of love; she wanted to preserve the relationship. However, after she raised the subject, her parents doubled down. The fresh guilt, condemnation, and fear they heaped on her nearly derailed her healing process as she became riddled with unbearable anxiety.

If a sufferer's environment is unsafe and they desire a confrontation with the person who is harming them, help them to find a place to stay if things do not go well or encourage them to delay the confrontation until they have more stability in other areas, such as economic stability, even if that may take months. There was ample evidence to suggest that Katie's parents were going to escalate their abuse if confronted. If the steps above had been taken in her situation, Katie would have been better protected and able to heal.

At the same time, be aware that some situations are too dangerous for a victim to remain in and may even be potentially lethal. In these cases, urge them not to confront their abuser and plead with them to flee to safety. If you suspect someone you are working with is in such a situation, have someone with experience help them to prepare a safety assessment and plan.

Work toward physiological stability. At the outset, take great care to attend to a victim's ongoing physical distress. People are embodied souls, and we should work to stabilize their bodies before we lean into their inner distress. Does this person struggle to sleep normally, have trouble eating, or experience anxiety or depressive symptoms? If so, would medical interventions be helpful for alleviating their symptoms? What lifestyle changes might be beneficial for them?

If you start your journey with this person long after the initial trauma, check for chronic physical issues that may need to be addressed. Have they developed harmful ways of managing distress that work against their healing process (such as substance use)? Are they engaged in dangerous behaviors (such as driving too fast or having promiscuous sex)? Are they wrestling with suicidal ideation? Help them to see that their current strategies are destructive, and work toward the longer-term goal of turning to the Lord when they are distressed.

Determine relational stability. Due to the nature of trauma, many victims are isolated and commonly avoid other people. It is natural for sufferers to isolate themselves in order to avoid reminders or aggravation of current or past pain. And if a sufferer's trauma stems from abuse, it was likely perpetrated by someone in their family or church. This has a particularly dramatic impact on a sufferer's relationships.

Because trauma work often involves lifting a person's shame and guilt and restoring their trust, it is helpful to assess their relational landscape early. Learn whose voices influence them (Prov. 13:20). Are they walking with wise companions or with fools? Victims are often pressured or persuaded by others to adopt an unhelpful narrative to explain what happened to them. For example, one of Emily's friends kept telling her that if she had only broken up with her boyfriend after their last argument, she would not have been assaulted by him. Emily felt paralyzing guilt even though she had done nothing wrong.

Find out if the sufferer has a support system. Could any current relationships be a potential detriment to their healing process? Do they know someone spiritually wise who can support them with prayer (James 5:16)?

If the person you are working with has healthy relationships, help them to think creatively about how to make good use of them (Eccl. 4:10). Not everyone in their life will know how to assist them with their trauma, but some will be great prayer warriors, and others might simply have a ministry of presence and be companions who can go on walks, enjoy movies, and eat meals with them.

Assess spiritual stability. Before you engage too deeply in spiritual matters with trauma victims, you need to know how their relationship with God has been impacted. Almost all victims wrestle with questions like the following:

- "How could the Lord let this happen to me?" (see Ps. 44:9)
- "Does he see my anguish?" (see Ps. 44:24)
- "I have been faithful, so why is this happening to me?" (see Ps. 44:17-19)
- "Will the Lord help me?" (see Ps. 44:23)

Some victims, like Emily, make unbiblical connections about what has happened to them.

Emily believed God had used this traumatic event to punish her because he was displeased that she had recently cut off communication with her father. Such ways of thinking make it hard for victims to see the Lord's pursuit and care of them.

In the early stages of care, our goal is to simply gain an awareness of how a sufferer's faith has been affected. Later we can progress to helping them use the psalms to express their anguish to God.

For now, don't assume. Be reassuring and gentle as you ascertain how a person is doing spiritually. Find out if they can pray, attend church, read their Bible, enjoy worship music, or go to their small group. It is likely that they will experience challenges with these spiritual practices, so heed the words of Jude to "have mercy on those who doubt" (v. 22) as you learn about any struggles. Listen attentively for ways victims talk about the Lord and give them permission to share their questions (Ps. 34:18). Invite them to speak about any promises or passages in Scripture that bring them hope or leave them feeling condemned.

Finally, note that the impacts of trauma on a person's faith are not always negative. I'm often left in awe when a sufferer testifies to the Lord's care of them through their trials (Rom. 5:3–5).

Screen for self-harm and suicide risk. Some trauma victims deliberately injure themselves.

The most common type of self-harm is cutting, but it can take other forms: burning, scratching, carving words into the skin, hitting oneself, banging one's head against a hard surface, piercing the skin, picking at wounds, and pulling one's hair.

People self-harm for a variety of reasons. They may do so to process their negative feelings, distract or punish themselves, elicit pain when they feel numb, or express emotions that they are embarrassed to show. For some, self-harm may give a false sense of control.

Sometimes the pain of trauma leaves a person feeling so hopeless that they imagine the only end to the pain is death. We can understand why they might see their death as the only escape from a suffering that currently feels so intense. However, thoughts of death can escalate to actual plans for how to die, so ask the person if they are wrestling with thoughts about suicide.[5]

Because counseling stirs up painful memories for victims, it is important to develop healthy strategies for how they can handle their distress *before* you ask them to engage deeply in counseling. Otherwise, any of their harmful behaviors might be intensified. For example, a childhood sexual abuse victim, Cathy, struggled after our sessions with flashbacks of her abuse, but she kept them to herself. When I asked her about flashbacks, she minimized their frequency and paralyzing impact on her. In time, I learned that she would burn herself in the shower after counseling to numb the pain that surfaced with her memories. To unearth such situations, be sure to ask the person how they process their emotions after they speak with you.

Establish a plan of response. To some degree, trauma victims are usually unsafe and unstable in several areas until they are well into their healing journey. In your early days with them, brainstorm strategies for how they can endure challenges well.

In regard to physical symptoms like sleeplessness, panic attacks, and the inability to eat, identify practical ways your counselees can calm themselves, release stress, restore sleep, distract themselves appropriately, manage their pain, fight against the temptation to self-harm, and gain strength for the journey ahead.[6] Those whose relationship with God is intact will be able to lean into prayer; their faith and Scripture will help them. Others may first need to be stabilized physiologically so that they are able to engage with God and his Word. A wonderful way they can learn to seek God's care for them is by praying for their physical relief.

Even if the sufferer is not currently responding to the trauma in destructive ways, be proactive to address any intrusive thoughts and emotions. For example, as Tom began talking to an elder about a deadly fire, he remembered more details from that night and his head filled with people's cries for help. Tom needed to address his intrusive memories of people screaming.

God invites us to "be still, and know that I am God" (Ps. 46:10)—to orient ourselves to him. It often takes time to quiet distressing thoughts. Sufferers may benefit from practical helps to slow down their thoughts—for example, journaling, praying with a friend, or engaging their minds in other tasks, such as reading books or going for walks.[7] Help them to identify God as their impermeable refuge and to direct their thoughts to him. This will bear fruit in their bodies as well.

Although not all sufferers need a concrete plan, some may benefit from writing one out. I have included a sample plan at the end of this booklet so that you can help sufferers to prepare one for themselves.

How you address a survivor's safety and stability will significantly affect how they walk through the healing process. So, as counseling progresses or as new layers of suffering are exposed, circle back and reassess how a sufferer is doing in any areas you noted might be hard for them, and revise their written plan as needed.

3. Build Trust as Their Guide
The third foundation of trauma care is to build trust between yourself and the sufferer. If

you are unable to do this, the helping relationship *will* fall apart. As we have seen, trauma diminishes a person's ability to sustain relationships with God and others. In the case of sexual abuse in particular, the victim's ability to trust is shattered because they usually knew and trusted the abuser. In situations involving a horrific event such as terrorism or a combat experience, a person might wrestle with whether God cares for them and has good purposes for their life. Any traumatic experience will also affect their ability to relate to you, even though you are trying to help.

Therefore, plan to build trust. A sufferer is inviting you to see some of the most vulnerable parts of their being. If you are counseling in a formal setting, you often start your relationship as strangers, so it is good to go slowly. But even when you know the person already, you will still have to deepen your relationship. If they are to heal, they will need to trust the counsel, care, and suggestions you offer them as their guide.

Some victims retreat after sharing intimate details of their suffering. They feel overexposed and uncomfortable. Or the trauma can feel like it is happening all over again. This is how it was for Susan after she mentioned the sexual abuse she experienced when she was eight years old. She shared before the counseling relationship had been fully established. Because insufficient trust had been built, she was too uncomfortable to return to counseling.

How can we become trustworthy guides as we are counseling others? We have already seen how crucial it is that we understand trauma and its impacts well. But in addition we must strive to be humble and godly and to know *each individual sufferer* well so we can adapt our care to best help them.

Let's get more specific.

Know the sufferer well and mold your process to their needs. My friend who helped me to scale the waterfall was a trustworthy guide because she was able to calm *my* particular fears and take into account *my* particular vulnerabilities. It is critical for you to know and understand the person you are helping. You must keep in mind that they are not just a fellow traveler but someone who depends on your guidance. God has entrusted them to you, and they are particularly vulnerable and sensitive to your words and assessments.

I have been tempted to listen to a victim just long enough to bring them words to help them "get over" what happened—but not long enough to be a true help to them. I've had to learn to *slow down* and let things unfold at their pace. Then, and only then, am I equipped to help them move forward with assistance that is specific to their needs.

Part of molding your process to the needs of a sufferer involves thinking about how to care for the person holistically. Trauma disorganizes someone's inner world, challenges their relationship with God, and strains and stresses their body. A trustworthy guide knows how to navigate the terrain that lies ahead because they have learned about these impacts ahead of time and are ready to accurately apply what they have learned to a particular person.

Be willing to be flexible as you learn more about an individual's needs and the things that comfort them. Some of my counselees snuggle up under a blanket on the couch in my office or hold a warm cup of tea. A colleague has a therapy dog in her sessions. One survivor of sexual abuse would sketch while we talked. Another preferred for us to speak on a walk so that she could keep her whole body moving. Consider different ways to provide comfort as the person shares their story with you.

Learn about the benefits, weaknesses, and dangers of various interventions.[8] Research and find a trusted psychiatrist who can assess a sufferer's need for medication, and become familiar with other types of trauma interventions so you can speak wisely about them. A few of my counselees tried a therapy known as EMDR, and it significantly helped some of them with their recurring traumatic memories.[9] For others, it yielded mixed or no results. But in order to interact wisely with my counselees about EMDR, I had to first learn about it.

Know where you are headed. Your long-term goal is to help sufferers to flourish in their love for God and others. Even as you help a trauma victim to find relief from suffering, your primary goal is always to restore them to full worship—to a place where they are engaged day by day to live out the greatest commandment: "You shall love the Lord your God with all your heart and with all your soul and with all your mind" (Matt. 22:37).

You want them to trust and believe that they are loved, embraced, and protected by the Lord (Rom. 8:35, 37–39). That they are created for community (Gen. 2:18; Rom. 12:4–5). And that their gifts and service give God glory (1 Peter 4:10–11). This goal will not be fully realized until glory, but the wounds of the traumatized person should cause you to see their small steps up the steep terrain as heroic. When you know where you are headed and commit to getting there, you will counsel others with your eyes fixed on the Lord.

Be humble. As you learn more about the suffering of the person you are working with, you will be stretched and, at times, overwhelmed. You may wonder, "Am I doing everything I can? Is God at work? Any progress we make seems so slow. Can I really help this person heal?" I have had many moments of doubt as I've counseled complex cases. God has helped me by making it abundantly clear that I am limited, but he is not.

I can entrust my counselee to his care of them. This means I can depend upon him for what lies ahead (Ps. 34:17; Isa. 40:31). I need to pray and depend on his guidance for my counseling and counselee. Without the Lord, we can do nothing (John 15:5). But Christ sent his Helper, the Holy Spirit, to enable us to serve him (John 16:7). There are no easy solutions to trauma, but we have a God we can trust with trauma.

Jesus's love and care for his people is characterized by humility. He does not stand over his people but reaches out his hand tenderly as he comes to the aid of the sick and broken (Matt. 8:3; 14:14; Mark 1:31, 41). We must put on the character of Christ to serve sufferers well. The attributes of kindness, humility, meekness, and patience are the essential characteristics of both a trustworthy guide and a wise biblical counselor (Col. 3:12).

Be hopeful. It is easy to get discouraged on a hard journey, and much of the current trauma literature doesn't increase our hope. But no matter what wounds trauma leaves on a person's brain or body or soul, a simple truth remains: the most important shaping factor in a sufferer's story will always be Jesus and his redemptive work. Although this does not mean that all the impacts of trauma will be resolved in this life, we can be hopeful even amid trauma, because we place our hope in Christ.

You will at times be tempted to think otherwise. You might think that a person's trauma is too severe or that their faith will never flourish. But having hope means asking how they might live dependent upon Jesus, *even while* they are plagued with anxiety or other after-effects of the trauma (Matt. 11:28). We must be attentive to how Jesus is reshaping them, even if it's at an excruciatingly slow rate—by paying attention to this, we lean into hope. Hope for what God can do changes our trajectory and our counsel (James 1:2–4, 12; 1 Peter 5:10; 2 Peter 1:3–4).

Trauma victims often wrestle with the question "Who can I trust?" If you can be the kind of guide described above, they will likely trust you. Trust is a rare commodity for someone who has been traumatized. Treasure it.

Jesus: The Most Trustworthy Guide

In this booklet we've seen that the impacts of trauma are vast and that they require comprehensive care. While there is much to consider, ultimately the most important thing we need do is to emulate our Lord and Savior. Our counsel depends upon and points to the perfect Guide. He is gentle and humble, and he walks at the pace that a hurting person needs. He guides us as we guide survivors. A good guide follows him because he knows the way.

We may be Jesus's hands and feet, but ultimately *he* is the one who leads people out of their wilderness. His ascent out of the valley of death provides a secure pathway for us to follow. His journey makes ours possible. The promise found in Psalm 121:7–8—"The LORD will keep you from all evil; he will keep your life. The LORD will keep your going out and your coming in . . . forevermore"—takes on a new meaning in Jesus. It is not that we are immune to evil, but we can trust we will not be consumed by it. He is the Great Shepherd of Israel, whose protection, guidance, and blessing move his people to the ultimate place of safety.

Bonus Resource: A Plan for Finding Refuge in Moments of Distress

When I was working with Emily, we brainstormed constructive places of refuge for her. Our goal was to stabilize her during times of distress so that she would be better able to connect to the Lord when they happened. Here's the plan we used.

1. **I can tell I am in distress when . . .** [For example, a sufferer might answer *I haven't slept for more than three hours, I cry when driving to work,* or *I don't answer phone calls from good friends.*]
2. **What warning signs indicate I may be about to turn to a poor strategy for**

managing my distress? [Often you will have to help the sufferer to make connections between their distressing thoughts, emotions, and situations and the places and behaviors they turn to for comfort. For Emily, warning signs included looking online for ways to cut herself, restricting what she was eating, and exercising excessively.]

3. **Here are three ways I can change my thoughts in the moment:** [Exploring these options can also help you to better get to know the person you are caring for as you discover that they are comforted by listening to a certain podcast or working on a hobby.]

4. **What are some ways I can comfort my body when it is reacting to triggers for my trauma?** [Some survivors of trauma may experience bodily symptoms such as panic attacks. Some helpful self-soothing techniques include using breathing exercises, going on walks, or lying down and thinking about relaxing at the beach.]

5. **Whom can I call or text to help me reset my focus?** [When a survivor is distressed, whom can they connect with in order to take themselves out of a spiral?]

6. **Where can I go to focus my attention on something else?** [This question refers

to a physical location, such as a craft store, bookstore cafe, or local park.]

7. **Whom can I call and wisely entrust with my story?** [This question prompts great conversations about whom a survivor can trust with their heart. If you have concerns about someone they mention based on what they have already shared, gently mention this to them.]

8. **What do I need to change about my environment to keep me safe?** [For example, Emily needed to remove sharp objects that she thought about cutting herself with and avoid photographs of her friends' weddings, since the photographs fed her fears that she would not be able to find someone who would love her after her assault. On the positive side, Emily was also helped by writing Bible verses on her bathroom mirror.]

9. **What are life-giving ways I can find comfort?** [For example, the survivor might keep a journal to record the ways God is helping them, do gentle exercise, and make plans each week so that they are not home alone every night.]

10. **Bible verses that bring me comfort:** [It's important to encourage the person to generate verses on their own—even a phrase from Scripture.]

11. **How can I ask God to help me?** [Think about ways that God can help with small steps that you and the sufferer are working toward, such as falling asleep and staying asleep through the night or having the courage to talk about what happened.]
12. **If the intensity of my distress continues to rise, I will . . .** [If the strategies listed above are not sufficient to bring down the sufferer's distress, a good next step is often for them to reach out to their counselor.]

Darby A. Strickland counsels and teaches at the Christian Counseling & Educational Foundation (CCEF). She is the author of Is It Abuse? A Biblical Guide to Identifying Domestic Abuse and Helping Victims *and other books and articles.*

Worksheet: A Plan for
Finding Refuge in Moments of Distress

1. I can tell I am in distress when . . .

2. What warning signs indicate I may be about to turn to a poor strategy for managing my distress?

3. Here are three ways I can change my thoughts in the moment:

4. What are some ways I can comfort my body when it is reacting to triggers for my trauma?

5. Whom can I call or text to help me reset my focus?

6. Where can I go to focus my attention on something else?

7. Whom can I call and wisely entrust with my story?

8. What do I need to change about my environment to keep me safe?

9. What are life-giving ways I can find comfort?

10. Bible verses that bring me comfort:

11. How can I ask God to help me?

12. If the intensity of my distress continues to rise, I will . . .

Notes

1 The stories in this book are true. However, names and identifying details have been changed to protect the privacy of the individuals involved.

2 Darby Strickland and Ed Welch, "Trauma: Bearing the Unbearable," Regional Conference Audio (2019), https://www.ccef.org/shop/product/trauma-bearing-the-unbearable-digital-download/. See also Diane Langberg, *Suffering and the Heart of God: How Trauma Destroys and Christ Restores* (Greensboro, NC: New Growth Press, 2015) and Bessel van der Kolk, *The Body Keeps the Score: Brain, Mind, and Body in the Healing of Trauma* (New York: Viking Penguin, 2014).

3 Complex trauma occurs when a person is exposed to multiple traumatic events that tend to be severe, long-term, invasive, and interpersonal in nature. The complexity comes from the nature of the multiple sources and the longer duration of harm. Violence, abuse, and neglect are common sources of complex trauma. Children are most vulnerable to complex trauma.

4 For a safety plan that addresses protecting children while a victim remains in the home or is fleeing abuse, see Darby A. Strickland, *Is It Abuse? A Biblical Guide to Identifying Domestic Abuse and Helping Victims* (Phillipsburg, NJ: P&R Publishing, 2020), or contact the National Domestic Violence Hotline: www.thehotline.org.

5 For guidance on suicide assessment, see Aaron Sironi and Michael R. Emlet, "Evaluating a Person with Suicidal Desires," *Journal of Biblical Counseling* 26, no. 2 (2012): 33–41. In addition, a helpful web page is "Screen/Access," Zero Suicide, accessed June 6, 2023, https://zerosuicide.edc.org/toolkit/identify/screening-options.

6 For an example of how to address bodily symptoms in biblical counseling, see Todd Stryd, "'Take a Deep Breath'—How Counseling Ministry Addresses the Body," *Journal of Biblical Counseling* 32, no. 3 (2018): 62–74.

7 For a biblical and practical resource to help sufferers address their intrusive thoughts, see Esther Smith, *A Still and Quiet Mind: Twelve Strategies for Changing Unwanted Thoughts* (Phillipsburg, NJ: P&R Publishing, 2022).

8 Edward T. Welch, "Trauma and the Body: An Introduction to Three Books," *Journal of Biblical Counseling* 33, no. 2 (2019): 61–83.

9 EMDR stands for Eye Movement Desensitization and Reprocessing therapy. It is a psychotherapy that seeks to reduce the intensity and emotions associated with traumatic memories. It uses bilateral eye movements as the person receiving care focuses on a traumatic memory. The Biblical Counseling Coalition released a statement on EMDR that is a great starting place for learning how some in the biblical counseling world think about it. It is important to note that some biblical counselors would make stronger statements cautioning against EMDR while others are more open to it. I do not wish to enter that debate here. I simply want to offer a starting place for learning about it: "BCC Statement on EMDR," Biblical Counseling Coalition, December 16, 2021, https://www.biblical counselingcoalition.org/2021/12/16/bcc-statement-on-emdr/ and "What Is EMDR?" EMDR Institute, Inc., accessed June 6, 2023, https://www.emdr.com /what-is-emdr/.

ALSO BY DARBY A. STRICKLAND

God does not intend for marriage to be a place of oppression. Providing practical tools and exercises, biblical counselor Darby Strickland prepares potential helpers to pick up on cues that could point to abuse and to explore them wisely. You will learn how to identify a range of abusive behavior and better understand the impact of abuse on victims—particularly wives. Ultimately, you will become equipped to provide wise and Christ-centered counsel while navigating a difficult and complex situation.

"*Is It Abuse?* is a stunning work. It is brave without being incendiary. It is carefully and thoroughly biblical. It is relentlessly practical. . . . If you ever read a book about abuse in couples, let it be this one."
–Alasdair Groves, Executive Director, Christian Counseling & Educational Foundation

ALSO BY DARBY A. STRICKLAND

In *Domestic Abuse: Help for the Sufferer*, experienced family counselor Darby Strickland helps those oppressed by abuse to speak out, find support, and determine their next steps, showing God's heart for them and desire to rescue them.

Writing to counselors, friends, and family in *Domestic Abuse: Recognize, Respond, Rescue*, Strickland describes what truly happens in oppressive marriages and shows helpers how they can defend and protect victims while correcting and discipling abusers.

RCL Ministry Booklets

Booklets by Jeffrey S. Black, Michael R. Emlet, Walter Henegar, Robert D. Jones, Susan Lutz, James C. Petty, David Powlison, Darby A. Strickland, Paul David Tripp, Edward T. Welch, and John Yenchko.

See all the books and booklets in the Resources for Changing Lives series at www.prpbooks.com